To Brooke,
I hope you enjoy
the poems.

♡

T 〜 W.
Wright

Rodeo of the Soul

Poems by Daniel W. Wright

Spartan Press

Kansas City   Missouri

Spartan Press

Kansas City, MO

spartanpresskc@gmail.com

Spartan
Press

So many people to thank! Firstly, to Jason Ryberg and everyone at Spartan Press. Thanks for believing in the material in this book. Next round is on me in St. Louis (or Kansas City, which comes first)! I also want to say a big thanks to Sarah Weeks and Sara Hussain for their help in editing the book. A shout out to the Livery Company, the best damn dive bar in the mid-west. A big thanks to Clyde Always, the Bard of the Lower Haight, and Café International in San Francisco. Thanks for always making me feel welcome. To John Patrick Robbins and the *Rye Whiskey Review.* Thanks for making my poems feel at home! And finally, much love to my blood family, my South City family, and my poet family. See you all around soon!

A few of the poems in this collection have appeared in *Gasconade Review, Bad Jacket,* and *The Rye Whiskey Review*

CONTENTS

Rodeo of the Soul / 1

Rumble / 3

All Good Things / 5

I'm Gone / 7

A Poem for You / 9

Aftermath of a Series of Rejection Letters / 11

There's a Sucker Born Every Minute / 14

Omit the Logic / 15

In Another Time... / 18

Planet News / 20

House Show / 21

The Universe and I / 23

The Toy / 24

Passion / 25

Any Minute Now / 27

Sending Out Hank / 29

Break a Leg / 30

The Flags Were at Half Mast / 31

Drink Like Old Hollywood / 32

Stalled Engine / 34

Five Steps Back / 37

Past Due / 39

You're Not Worth the Jail Time / 40

Lunch Break / 43

A Dog's Life / 44

Viva La Revolution? / 46

Through A Door / 47

Invisible Conversation / 48

Two Drunks / 49

Notes from an American Love Letter / 50

Jackpot / 54

The Typewriter / 55

On the Cooler / 56

Bomb Scare / 57

No Pictures, Please / 59

Summer / 61

I Was Told / 63

Cards You're Dealt / 65

Let Me Tell You a Thing or Three / 67

808's and Snowflakes / 69

Dedicated to Bill Christman, Deana Hegel, Joe Schwartz, Greg Bynum, Stephanie Von Drasek, and Tim Ryan.

Thanks for the lessons.

Dear Dan –

*As the Bohemian torch bearer to the 21st century –
you must remember that all the noblest ventures to elevate
humanity will be misunderstood (at best) and snuffed out
violently more often! I refer you to my heroes: JFK, RFK,
MLK, Malcolm X, Tom Merton, etc.*

Ergo my foolish friend –

ONWARD TO OBLIVION!

-Big Bill

Rodeo of the Soul

I see egos run like wild horses
never knowing which way to turn
and trampling over so much
Friends you've turned into false prophets
make you want to run away
to have a moment
to yourself

Innocent stories
cause you trouble
when you tell them to people
who haven't lived
Sense of humor is left in the cigarettes
you can't smoke anymore

Someone call me a dream
as I dive in moonlit waves
to let the world leave me be
I'll always feel for ol' Cherokee
but now I must search
for somewhere I can go
where no one knows
my mask of shame

Rants come first
and poetry comes later

Bullets start wars
as words try to end them
The rodeo of the soul
tells you of divine mysteries
begging to be discovered
Where stars and wind
flow through your hair
as you search in the cracked windows
of warehouse eyes
for answers to questions
that haven't been asked

Never letting yourself up
only brings you down
Overwhelming silence
is all you hear
when it all
comes crashing down

Hibernation is not allowed
Nation more woke
than a Spike Lee joint
After peace of mind
comes peace of soul

Rumble

Type your poem so loud
that you wake up your roommate

Scream it out so loud
that you gain a drunk's attention

Beat it out so long
that your heart syncs up to its rhythm

Let it change you so much
that you leave the husk of who you were on the floor

Yearn for it so much
that you're not ashamed to cry

Do not leave it alone
until you know who you stare at in the mirror

Never let it sit
idly in your mind
only to fade away with other forgotten thoughts

Write it down
Even if it's the dumbest thing
you ever thought

If it brought something out of you
a laugh or an eye roll
it's worth something

You and your misery
are never as alone as you think

All Good Things

(A Poem For A Jaded Optimist)

Black shoes
black shirt
but never a black heart
Friends may come and go
Lovers may come and go
but despite it all
I still love

An awkwardness makes me
keep the world
at a distance
while love and loneliness
make me want to hold it close
Too much love
is never enough
I just wish
we could all be better
to each other

Some call me depressed
I call me a realist
Some call me a cynic
I call me a jaded optimist

But by being an optimist
others want to call you stupid
Though humanity
loves to show its demons
there is an angel
Doing little things
that go a long way

I'm always on the lookout
for those little things
so I can have
an honest reason to smile
and even amongst
End of Day feelings
I can still feel
this pale blue dot
is worth saving

I'm Gone

I tried so long to preach truths
but truths only got me
what you'd expect
I'm not ready to preach lies
just yet
But I will rewrite
a couple of forgotten bromides
and sign my name to them

I see children run down streets
Mad in love
Sainted hotels stare across the street
at sainted hospitals
So many want to be the ghost;
most are lucky just to be an echo

Chaos comes in many forms
Only some of them accept you
Within me
there's the fan
the watcher
the ladies man
the loser
All begging to be invisible
in an age
where all must be accounted for

Staring into a mirror
knowing that who I am when I wake up
and who I am when I lay my head down
are always two different people

Heads on fire
No true souls
Everyone has a nail and cross
I know mine fairly well
God save the secrets that you know
Rainbow shined yesterday
Politicians die the moment they speak
People want the world under their thumb
I change my mask every day
that I remember to

I'm really quite simple
I'm just a bunch of rants and rambles
Here one second
gone the next.

A Poem For You

Keep this close to your heart
Never let them see
A poem meant for your eyes only
I'll give you words
both heartfelt and sardonic
so you won't know what's real
I hope it's not a bother
I don't want to make life any more difficult
than what you tell me

I don't expect you
to magically change your mind
I know a poem
doesn't change a thing
I don't expect this poem
to do anything
except explain a dream
I don't want to wake up from

I'll give you honesty
because that's what you've given me
and even if you haven't
I never knew
and probably wouldn't have cared anyway
I'll give you respect
because the way you tell it

those others give you none
and to me
you deserve a hell of a lot more
than that

I'll give you everything
someone in my position can
but only once
because anybody who repeats themselves
isn't worth anything

So here it is
everything in one poem
except my heart
because I'm not ready
and neither are you

Aftermath of a Series of Rejection Letters

The first rejection came in an envelope
from something that called itself
the Toilet Paper Review
I remember submitting to them
because I liked their slogan:
We Give a Shit
The envelope had all of the poems
I had sent them
along with a note that said simply
These poems ARE shit.
All things considered,
I didn't know
if I should take that
as a bad thing
with them.

The next rejection
came from a magazine in California.
They called themselves *Rattled Cage*.
They said my poems were good
but I just cared about too much.
They then thanked me
for sending them
and ten minutes later
sent a second e-mail

wherein they apologized
for not getting a chance
to read any of them.

After that
was a printing company
who said they were interested
in publishing a novel I had written.
They said they liked the novel
but it was too short,
too idealistic,
too romantic,
they didn't like the development
of the main character
and were curious
if I could change the setting
from St. Louis
to anywhere else.
Couldn't you change it
to somewhere more appealing?
Like, say,
Cincinnati?

The final rejection
came two days later
in an e-mail.
It was a literary review
based in New York.

They said
that from reading my poems,
one would think
I have a drinking problem.
They then thanked me
for submitting to them
and asked if I'd like to pay
to subscribe to their magazine.
No thanks, I replied
I need the money for drinking.

After that,
I took all of the rejections,
crumpled them up
and threw them in the trash.
Not knowing what else to do,
I opened a beer and drank it.
Then, I put a piece of paper
in the typewriter
and started all over.

There's a Sucker Born Every Minute

All the nobodies
you were convinced were somebodies
all melt away
when they stretch themselves
so thin
they become transparent

They will see you
for what you are
before you do
and offer you the kind of fun
that only turns into pettiness
trying to convince you
that the only way to live
is to drown yourself
in the unnecessary

When you find out who you are
that's when you find out
who they are
and that's when they'll run away
That's when they'll find
a new best friend
There's a sucker born
every minute

Omit the Logic

Omit the logic
let the world have its myths
When romanticism fades
Reality's a whiskey you can't afford
When you don't have too much
you won't get too far
but everyone wants
to get their dime

Different wavelengths
confuse those
who don't comprehend
Crossroads in Mexico
take you to the same road
where cheap fencing
keeps border patrols company
Trying to focus on your mind
while drunk regulars
pound on guitars
Passion can only take you
so far in a song
but three chords can take you further
Take the pin out of the foundation
watch the building fall
let the new guard build with the remains

Omit all logic
say what you want to say
words are just weapons
that can settle anything
when put in the right order
Violence is their game
because they don't understand yours
as they realize that
a suit of armor to protect themselves
against apple cider vinegar
seems a bit much
but what do you expect
when billy clubs
make up for penis size
When dealing with everyone
from the commander in chief
to your local police officer
omit all logic
omit all reason
and see then if things make sense

The heart is not made to withstand
21st century pacifism
When it is filled with 20th century passion
Torn between high touch and high tech
Love is in my mind but freedom is in my soul
The voice of poets are powerful enough
to scare fascists

If love of beauty is the path to Hell
then what is the point
of the beauty of Heaven?

World's a Dali painting
wrapped in an Escher staircase
Phobias upload the moment I wake
like a phone that refuses to break
Body is pained but I feel fine
Daily problems I write about never disappear
Pills I'm offered have no effect on me
as freedom stands
beyond comfortable boundaries
Insanity makes sense
when it breaks you
when you omit all logic

In Another Time...

In another time
I could see you smile in Parisian rain
looking as beautiful as a painting
jumping in puddles while holding an umbrella

In another life
I could see us living in domestic bliss
where everything would've fit in place
and we could both be happy

In another place
all of our friends
wouldn't be able to think of one of us
without thinking of the other
In another time
it all would've been right

In another world
I would know all the right things to say
I wouldn't be scared of truths I can't face
We could take care of each other
when we were sick
we could lift the other
when they were down

In another universe
We could allow ourselves
to believe in silly things
like soul mates and true love
which only become silly
when you become too jaded
to ever trust again

Somewhere out there
we are together
we are happy
we give each other love and encouragement
and I never had to write this poem
I wish I was there

Planet News

The problem with the revolution
being televised
is that that's when everyone
turns off their television

History has shown
that there is no such thing
as extraordinary men and women
Just ordinary men and women
in extraordinary situations
Though we were told history ended
when Berlin dropped its wall
it continues to unfold
in ways
that scare so many

When time pulls back the curtain
people run like roaches
in the light
while junkies
declare themselves emperor
World warned
to be on the brink
but no more than it was
fifty years ago

House Show

The guitar matches the flame
False endings bring smiles
Dylan poetry used in response
to questions
are met with rolled eyes
Lyrics shine
like champagne and heartache

Claps and snaps
encourage tales
of honesty confused
for stars
Buddha lamp sheds light
on hipster hi tops
that rub together

Pinky fingers look like lit cigarettes
in a certain light
Beer bottles clank too loudly
as people make whiskey faces
out of embarrassment
Young fanboys now old
wish to travel through time
and dance to suicidal odes
of lost loves

Salt and pepper beards
make conversation
with long hair under ski caps
Back row snickers amongst itself
like naughty kids in school
Collage smiles in the dark
Peace in the neighborhood
A drink keeps you company
when you don't know anyone else

The Universe and I

Though talk cries apocalypse
I am not afraid
because life finds a way
even if it means
the end of us
Nothing that has been made
can ever truly
be destroyed

Our destinies
are in the cosmos
we'll get there some way
Our fate
is in our hands

Whatever comes next
is our doing
Whatever comes next
I'll make the best of it
Whatever comes next
will be another adventure

The Toy

The child bought the toy
not because they wanted it
not because they'd have fun with it
not because it sparked their imagination
but because they heard
that another child
wanted it

So now the toy sits on the shelf
collecting dust with a smile
half forgotten
except when the child sees it in passing
out the corner of their eye
and the child smiles
because no one else
has it

Passion

Passion inspired me
to go to the coast
where I gave a good reading
I invited Passion
out for drinks
but two hours
before we were supposed to meet
she said she couldn't come
laying blame
to a twenty-four hour illness
that suddenly sprung up

I wasn't too sad
because there were plenty of things
to do without Passion
still though
wish I could've seen her
if only for a few minutes

I still think of how Passion
came 2,000 miles
to see me read
and how sometimes
the greatest passion
can come
from not fucking

I miss Passion and wish her well
I would've used her real name
but I'll keep that
for myself

Any Minute Now

Any minute now
I'll be called back to a real world
as a world that seemed so real
begins to fade away
I'll belong again to a clear day
with a family picture
next to an office computer desk
and exploits of a fake life
written in a private file

Any minute now
I'll have a one-second embarrassment
as I realize I'm still a grown-up dreamer
who did nothing
I'll drive home to a happy life
that's empty
though inside of me
I can swing in on a chandelier

Any minute now
I'll come to my senses
as someone calls my name out
too loud
Every poem will become
just another forgotten good idea
and I'll think on
unreal memories

The world will be as I remember it
everyone else eating a three-course meal
while I'll be eating my licorice shoe
The Groucho Marxist poets will fade away
to where everything else imaginary goes
when playtime's over

But this dreamer wants
just one more roll of the dice
let the real world wait a little bit longer
any minute now
I know I can win

Sending Out Hank

The bookstore I work at
had an original Bukowski chapbook
worth $100
I sometimes took it out
and read the words of the old master
I wondered what he'd think
about his early day chapbooks
going for so much

One day an online order came in for the book
Before I sent it out
I took it with me to the bathroom
and read it
while I dealt with a good beer shit
from the night before

After I was done
I secured the book in packaging
Insured it
and then sent it off to Burbank, California
and somewhere
I heard Hank laugh

Break a Leg

Clap hands in an empty theatre
to let them know you're there
It don't matter if you play for no one
even if after weeks and weeks of promoting
to get a million maybes
and *can you get me in for free* friends
your only audience are the other performers
and their significant others
who stepped out for a smoke break
You never go onstage
because you're ready
you only go on
because it's time
Coughing here ain't ailment
It's criticism
because even Jesus knew
that no one respects you
in your hometown

Know your price
Never budge
Making it to me
may not be
making it
to you

The Flag Stands at Half-Mast

Men and women jump from too high
Airplanes crash into towers
Everything all falls down in World History class
while just the day before
we had learned of the fall of the Roman Empire

When playtime's over
the fangs come out
and we feast on dreams, myths and legends
telling anyone younger than us
that they're doomed
to boredom
and the end of the world

Loose lips sink ships
Paranoia higher than threat levels
Christian Jihadists
and Muslim fundamentalists
both get flipped
at random intervals
as two sides of the same coin

Some get lucky
find a friend to calm them down
Others find a gun
and the flag stands at half-mast

Drink Like Old Hollywood

We should all be so lucky
To drink
like old Hollywood drunks
We're all amateurs
by comparison

Drinking nothing stronger
than gin
before breakfast
or being able
to call a bachelor pad
Cirrhosis by the sea

We would all be so honored
as to drink so much
that you woke up
in a Chicago asylum
or to know
you'd be buried
with six bottles of whiskey

We would all thank the gods
if we drank so much
we woke up the next day
married to Richard Burton
or Liz Taylor

To be a member
of the American Olympic drinking team
To drink so much
the on-set bar got shut down
by the head of the studio
To have so many stories
told about you
that nobody knows
which ones are true
Legends last longer anyway
We would all be so lucky

Stalled Engine

Worried I'll break the key
if I try any harder
too much to think about to focus
Worried I'm being too autobiographical
Worried I'm being too negative
Worried about a friend in the hospital
Worried about a friend who almost OD'd
Brain hurts when I jerk off
Too long since I wrote last poem
Sunshine and rainbows ain't coming today
Meditative mind asks who I'm trying to kid
Feels good to just write anything again
Owe too much money to too many people
The people understand
Uncle Sam does not
Too late to give fucks
Electronic crucibles
now new norm by amateur thought police
Doing good otherwise
Trying to avoid double talking smiles
who don't like their lives
so they have to ruin others

I love bad poetry
but only when I write it for myself

Tangents come on and tangents go off
Too much to say
I worry I'm not listening
like I used to
Feeling crowded
by overweight American Underbelly
wearing a shirt that says
Beer
Bacon
Guns
Freedom
Bragging *I'm just a ding dong away
from diabetes!*
With a black pickup truck
that sports a bumper sticker
that says *Ditch the bitch. Let's fish*
I bet his favorite tv station is ABC
because that's as much of the alphabet
as he can remember

The longer I stay in one spot
the more I feel my reputation
become two-dimensional
because it's easier for everyone else
as I'm put up in an ivory tower
I've been told I worked hard for
but never asked to have
As others toast to so-called geniuses

that they only acknowledge
because someone else said so

I feel boozed down
and fattened up
My ego made to believe
I'm untouchable
That's when they slip the noose
around my neck
And offer me as a sacrifice
to the Gods

One-way tickets
can't come soon enough
as life tries to take the excitement
out of good things
and tries to make me lost
in another forest
and to forget how to follow northern stars
that now somehow
don't seem to shine as bright
as they did a day ago

Five Steps Back

She accused me of not caring
after telling me that nothing mattered
She told me that when we slept together
it was only because she hadn't gotten any
in six months
and to not think too much
into anything that happened
She yelled at me
when I didn't message her the next day
She scolded me
when I was too exhausted to fuck her
She said I didn't care
She reminded me
that she was too good for me
despite her smelling like a drunk ashtray

She said that the feelings she felt
no man could ever understand
I guess that's fair
She complained about the other men
who wouldn't sleep with her
She made me not want to go
to bars that had been safe havens
because she'd cause a scene
whenever I didn't give her
what she wanted

She cried to me about how lonely she felt
how she just wanted to be held
as she drifted off to sleep
She tried to manipulate me
to give her what she wanted
making me feel guilty for
knowing the meaning of the word
no

She reminded me
of who I once was
but that only served to remind me
of who I am
She hinted towards suicide
and that made me cry
She threw everything inside herself
at me
not caring how I felt
She said I was lucky
that she ever bothered
to be interested in me again
Jury's still out on that one

Past Due

I sometimes wonder
what the bill companies
think of me

Another South City fuck
who can't pay his shit on time!
Can't wait to disconnect
that asshole!

That may be true
BUT
I always do pay my shit
It may take a Disconnection Notice
to do it
BUT
I still always
pay my shit

It's Not Worth the Jail Time

It's not worth the jail time
I have to remind myself of that fact
Every time I see you
No matter how much you may deserve it
For you attacking my friend
your now-ex
and attacking my roommate
who did nothing but defend you
I have to remind myself
You are not worth the jail time

The few friends you have left
want me to know how sorry you are
for doing all the things you do
That I should just get over it
though they seem unaware
that once the vase is broke
it can never be unbroke
But before I can say anything
you've done something else
and I shake my head
When does behavior stop being labeled
Just a quirk
and start being labeled
Destructive

I cringe
every time I see you
and ball my hand in to a fist
None of this is my fight
My friends can more than handle themselves
Yet I feel a need to say something
since no one else
is saying a damn thing

I'm not going to sit here
and pretend I'm tough
Any jail in the world
would eat me alive
But every time I see you
I wonder what it would be like if once
just once
I palmed your nose into your skull
Felt my fist upon your gut
Asked you how it felt
to be on the receiving end
or even take a baseball bat
and just go to town.
Not enough to kill you
but enough to let you know
to never lay a hand
on anyone I care for
ever
again

But then I shake my head
at those violent thoughts
and remind myself
You ain't worth the jail time
Hell
you're barely worth
this poem

Lunch Break

Leaves are turning
dollar for a banana
Hair too long for my taste
but money must go to food
Cars yell at other states' license plates
for not knowing how to drive

Perfect spot to sit in park
Not hiding
Just no one else here
Feeling fear of heights
staring at sky too long
Birds calling in earshot
Aloneness contents loneliness
Bugs go about their day

Leaves are turning
Wind gently ruffles my hair
Tree's shade is great company
Just out of view from the world
Not hiding
only waiting for the ones
who bother to look

A Dog's Life

Saw a small dog
being pushed in a stroller
with a huge smile on its face
and thought to myself
Man, that dog has it made
I bet its owner
picks up its shit
whenever it does its business
even at home
We should all be so lucky

I wonder if maybe that dog
thinks that it's the one in charge
It's not doing any chores
or heavy lifting
That when the owner leaves
it finds a stuffed animal
to have its way with
Whenever it makes a mess
the owner probably scolds the dog
in a tone of voice
usually used to tell
newborn babies
how cute they are

I'll bet anything
it probably gets the best dog food
money can buy
Maybe even a cooked steak
medium rare
every once in a while
It'll sit in its cozy home,
sleeping, eating, and shitting
without a care in the world

Maybe humans aren't the top
of the food chain
Dogs seem to have it
better than us

Viva la revolution?

Fingers point in every direction
at the accused
Line between Justice and paranoia
shorter than we think
History books are burned
by those who never read them
in French Revolution atmosphere
Good intentions make for perfect cover
It soon stops being about justice
and becomes people wanting to get rid
of the people we don't like
That's when we're all damaged

Through a Door

Every so often
the door at my job opens
and out of the corner of my eye
I swear I see you
for half a second
and get my hopes up
for just a little bit
that you're in town
for whatever reason

But then I see
that it's not you
It's only someone else
who looks partly like you
with the sun
shining perfectly behind them
to give off the sense of your aura

I can tell that they can sense
the hint of disappointment
in my voice
as I happily greet them
I know the truth of it is
that I'll probably never see you again
Not in any romantic way anyhow
I just wish we could realize the big moments
when they happen
instead of just living them

Invisible Conversation

I see a man across the street
sitting at an outside table
at a restaurant
yelling at the invisible person
sitting across from him

Whatever this invisible person has done
must be pretty bad as his voices gets louder and louder
pointing his finger as he drinks
saying *You know what you did! You know what you did!*

He goes back in the restaurant
and comes back out with a refill,
topping it off
with the flask
he pulls out of his pocket
Continuing to read his invisible companion
the riot act

He begins to nod his head
saying *I know, I know*
before calling bullshit
on some unknown subject
and then telling whoever it is sitting with him
It's all fun and games
until somebody bleeds!

Two Drunks

Two drunks
sharing beers
sharing songs
blues rock blares
over the bar
They're loud
they're the only ones here
They've got no worries
They've got no secrets
Two drunks at the bar
More free
than the rest of us

Notes from an American Love Letter

I want to love this country
like a madness
The fix may be in
and reality kayfabe
It's hard to grasp a war
when you've seen it all before
It's hard to believe
a word these days

But never tell an American the odds
because anything can be achieved
with a pair of dirty hands
Anything can be done
by sheer stubbornness
and an overwhelming desire
for better or worse
To prove the world wrong

We must fight on
we must
We must cry out
we must
We must look up
we must
We must keep hold
we must

Not allowed to be sick anymore
So many will work until their dying day
Do you wanna die
wearing that barista apron
wearing that red shirt and name tag
with a soccer mom
walking over your dead body
with co-workers you don't trust
being the ones who have to ID you
to the coroner
with a price gun in your hand
and over-homogenized Top 40
being the last sounds
you ever hear
as staff tries to be the first
to get to the break room
to get the lunch
you won't be eating anymore

Every guitar now
says it kills fascists
but none of them
ever fire a bullet
Good souls called out
get caught off-guard
stuttering when brain tries to run to the debate
and trips over its argument

We must find common ground
we must
We must see who's really at fault
we must
We must hold hands in solidarity
we must
We must do
we must

Sleeping on a floor
that's better than your bed
Getting angry at ignorance
yet still hoping love will conquer all
Though love never conquered
a damn thing
Unrequited love
is the American way

Wear your heart on your sleeve
if you can
We are all the marks
but it's still real to us
Day to day
nothing but 808s and snowflakes
With every McMurphy getting a lobotomy
free of charge
First line of defense can't hold
Second line of defense can't hold
So those who were told

they never had to pick up arms
attack the first two lines

Forgiveness from separated souls not enough
though there's more of us
than there are of them
The whole damn place is small
when it needs to be
but too damn big
to get the whole picture

If someone from the other side
ever tried to kill me
I would definitely fight
and run
and do
whatever I would have to do
to save my life in that moment
but now
I want them all to know
I love them
Not for ideology
but because they simply exist
I love them

We must see that there is still love
We must
We must
We must

Jackpot

I knew a guy
who had an accident happen to him
at his job
and the job gave him
a big settlement and two months' paid leave
just to make sure
he wouldn't sue

He took his settlement
and paid two months' rent on his place
and threw enough money at his utilities
to cover those same couple of months
Except for food
he didn't think to take food into account
he would take his weekly check
and he would say
Fuck it,
I'm spending this on good whiskey
and going to the track!

I asked him if he was going to go
to Fairmount Park
He said *Goddamn,*
that shithole's too dirty for even me!
I haven't seen him in a while
but I hope he made a killing
or at least found the best kind of whiskey
a man can drink

The Typewriter

I heard the faint sound
of a typewriter
as I laid in Limbo
aware that the awake world
lay beyond
one more door
but not ready for it yet
despite a need to check the time
so I didn't oversleep

I kept hearing the typewriter
somewhere in a distance
so I began to compose this poem
in my head
sitting in my kitchen at my Smith Corona
with no shirt or pants on
just my boxer briefs
and an ever loving need
to write

But as I typed
I fell back into the world of dreams
and it wasn't until
I was fully booted out
and awake
that I put this poem together
and somewhere in a distance
I still can hear
the typewriter

On the Cooler

Mystery monster people
Epic empty beautiful man
Happy for his villain heart
Magic love making
with some strange soul
Take me wisdom woman
my favorite voice and laugh

Come is the language of human desire
Crack from beneath
almost always a hero
More open story
that romance lives so short
Imagine another answer
through fiction

Bomb Scare

Two blocks of Grand
were blocked off
People who wanted
to get in to their apartment buildings
couldn't
Word was
there was a bomb scare

Well-dressed men
asked cops to make exceptions
to let them get their cars
that were just beyond
the yellow tape

The workers just beyond the yellow tape
silently feared for their lives
wondering if they were a safe distance away
from a potential blast
as they overheard customers
who had overheard cops

Passersby walking in the heat
complained to people
who weren't paying attention
about walking

an extra twenty feet
to take the back alleys
for two blocks
to get where they were going

In the end
it turned out
to be nothing
and people were more happy
about being able
to go to the gas station
to get a pack of smokes
than anything else

No Pictures, Please

No flash photography
or I won't go on
No clapping unless I give permission
or I won't go on
Don't use my picture to promote me
but please do pay me as much money
as I certainly think I'm worth
even though
this is merely a hobby for me
and the undercard care more
about their actual craft
than I do

Don't tell me the truth
or I won't go on
Though I am allowed to feel free
to tell you,
your business,
your staff,
and the other artists
how they tread upon my free spirit

Give me my roses before stage time
or I won't go on
Let me know everything is all right
or I won't go on

Please stroke my ego
and tell me I'm better
than the others

These are my terms and conditions
for performing tonight
You know how amazing I am
so sign on the dotted line
or I'll let everyone else know
about how much you hate
people like me

Summer

That street
is not my street anymore
and that's good
That's how it should be
We did good
with what time we had
so now it's their turn
Let the next generation
come along
Build it in their image

It's hard though
handing over
what you helped rebuild
what you owe so much to
Too many sunsets
that made you not worry so much
Too many drunken evenings
you danced away with best friends

Though this street
will be in the same spot
No matter how far one may travel
No matter how long one may stay away
It will never be
as you remember

because all things must pass
You must let go
But to let go
almost feels like letting go
of memories that formed
who and what you are
the person you are now
Thing you must remember
is that you are that person now
That street has done its job

Summer is never meant
to last forever

I Was Told

I was told I drank too much
before friends revealed
that it was partly their fault
because they didn't want to drink alone
and wanted to see
how far I could go

I was told that I put my arm
around a friend
and told them that we were surrounded
by Cthulu Walls
I was asked later what that meant
Fuck if I know

I was told I made an ass
of myself last night
as I kept running around
like a mad man
bar hopping between the three bars
on the same block
because each bar
had different people I knew

I was told that I laughed
as friends
punched me in the dick

in retaliation
for my
punching them in the dick

I was told I made it in time
to puke into the storm drain
because the bathrooms were full up
When I woke up the next day,
apparently I also puked
in front of my tv,
in the hallway,
in the toilet but didn't flush
and a little next to my bed

Wish I had a smart-ass thing
I could say about all this
But my head's still killing me
so I'm going back to bed

Cards You're Dealt

I wish I didn't have to write about politics
But the world we live in
doesn't make that an option anymore
I wish I was smarter than I am
so I could discuss policies
and political jargon
better than I do
I've always tried to approach politics
from a humanist perspective
but they've taken
what little humanity there was
out of the equation

They've taken humanity
out of a lot
I cry too much
as I try to keep up
with current events
I wish I could focus on peace and love
without feeling like I'm willfully
putting my head in the ground
The more I remain aware
the more claustrophobia sets in
even in wide open spaces

You don't have to like it
but you do have to accept
the cards you're dealt
I hope we can get a better hand
next round

Let Me Tell You a Thing or Three

You shouldn't drink
just to get fucked up
We're all fucked up enough
as it is
Go ahead
drink to numb the pain
but never forget it
Enjoy the night
It is full of possibilities
when you take off the blinders
that the work day put on you

If you don't have enough money
to tip the bartender
you shouldn't be at the bar
Buy a cheap beer if you want
but never be cheap
with the one
serving you your drinks

Always know your limits
never drink beyond them
unless you're ready
to face the next morning
Never blame anyone else

for your dumbass behavior
You drank
No one else forced you
End of story

808's and Snowflakes

I searched for enlightenment
but only found answers
I didn't want
Heal the truth
be the truth
Destiny arises
Solsbury Hill feeling
looking at neon red sunset
mixed with purple clouds
not the most beautiful
I've ever seen
but beautiful enough
to remind me of freedom

News reported
is already what you suspected
to be true
Fighting nonsense narcissist insults
for sake of basic human decency
Imaginary conversations with friends
where I'm at fault
confirm to me
that I'd leave this planet
at the first opportunity

Younger crowds coming in
blasting music any way they can
Don't know if I'm getting older
or if mainstream music just sucks
Minutiae escape in exhales
Wants of hope
Beer can't satisfy anymore
but still good time
with right company

College girls cozy up
to grey temples
Everyone's all dressed up
and too broke to go
Drunken cries for lost phones
to stay in touch
with toxic friends
Autumn and spring
fading into forever memory
People so afraid of responsibility
they call it *adulting*
People so afraid of love
they kill romance

Everyone knows how to rock
but they forgot how to roll
Trained to accept so little
that they forget to dream big

Walls seem so real
but only ever smoke and mirrors
They're just as human
as anybody else
Tear shed for old friends
Tear shed for old times
I hope to see them all again
down the road

Expatriate notions
more reality to consider
Solutions so simple
you cry when you think on them
We only want love
People pushed to darker ends
like lobsters in a Jacuzzi
A dozen years to clean up our act
it was fun while it lasted

Daniel W. Wright is a mid-western son who loves and loathes the red brick town that surrounds him. A poet of the no collar work force, Wright's work has appeared in the *Gasconade Review* as well as underground zines *Bad Jacket*, *Acid Kat*, and *Crappy Hour* as well as online reviews like *The Rye Whiskey Review*. His previous works include *The Death of the Ladies Man*, *Small Town Blues: Early Lyrics and Poems*, *Portrait*, *Murder City Special*, and *Working Bohemian's Blues*. Wright currently lives in St. Louis where you can usually find him in a bar or a bookstore.

This project was made possible, in part, by generous
support from the Osage Arts Community.

Osage Arts Community provides temporary time, space
and support for the creation of new artistic works in a
retreat format, serving creative people of all kinds —
visual artists, composers, poets, fiction and nonfiction
writers. Located on a 152-acre farm in an isolated rural
mountainside setting in Central Missouri and bordered
by ¾ of a mile of the Gasconade River, OAC provides
residencies to those working alone, as well as welcoming
collaborative teams, offering living space and workspace
in a country environment to emerging and mid-career
artists. For more information, visit us at www.osageac.org

Osage Arts Community

CPSIA information can be obtained
at www.ICGtesting.com
Printed in the USA
FSHW011440120519
58073FS